The Power of Positive Potty Pondering

The Power of Positive Potty Pondering

bathirmations

Affirmations designed to flush away life's burdensome loads while on the thinking pot

Lisa Z and Michelle Lang

Published by Lifermations LLC
Vancouver, WA

Lifermations LLC
Vancouver, Washington
www.lifermations.com

Bathirmations is a registered trademark of Lifermations LLC
Printed in the United States of America
ISBN: 978-0-9842888-1-6

Acknowledgments:
*Rock Creek Metal Craft (www.rockcreekmetalcraft.com)
for use of art in photos*
*River's Edge (www.riversedgeproducts.com) for use of
mini outhouses in photos*
*Interior photos by Lifermations LLC and Bonnie Stalberger
Photography © Lifermations LLC*
*Bathirmations logo designed by Stephanie Fisher and
Lifermations LLC*
Cover photo from Corbis.com
Editing by The Mighty Pen (www.mightypenediting.com)
Design by ALL Publications (www.ALLPublications.com)

Dedication

We dedicate this book to our families as their support and encouragement kept us moving in the right direction. You have been our inspiration and motivating force. This book is as much a result of your efforts as it is ours. We also want to give special acknowledgment to our dear friend, John Paris, for his unconditional support and faith in us and our work. His late wife, Peggy, had a wonderful sense of humor. She modeled how to live life to its fullest through her actions instead of through empty words. This little book is designed to help all of us put more action to our words with that same spirited sense of humor. Here is to you Peggy. Now, time to get this potty-party started.

Contents

Let's Get Moving

or . . .

Time to Get This Potty Started!

Have you ever pondered the thought that maybe obstacles are put in your way to help you on your journey through life? Is it possible that these challenges are designed to help you to learn more and to make you stronger? Is there any better use of bathroom time than affirming—or **bathirming**, if you will—who you are and who you want to be while on the thinking pot? What is bathirming you ask? In the simplest of terms, it's all about the art of letting go of both the emotional and physical impurities while using the bathroom, or more precisely, the toilet.

Let's face it. Everyone poops and it is no secret that many people like to read while sitting on the porcelain throne. This reading time may be more for the entertainment factor than for self-help reasons, but here is how it sits with us (or rather we sit on it): it's no coincidence that the word *toilet* is comprised of the words *to let* and right in the middle is an *I*. This obviously becomes *I let go*.

We challenge you to make better use of your letting-go time. Take a moment to simultaneously cleanse your inner self through the power of positive, or **poower** of **poositive**, thinking. Bathirm your way to better health, both emotionally and physically. Your emotional and physical health are strongly connected and each is dependent upon the other.

Think about this for a moment.

We as humans are made to move forward. Our knees bend forward, our arms swing forward, and so on. Now let's think about the part of our anatomy that stays, well, *behind*. You got it! We are designed to leave the physical and emotional impurities behind us and to move forward.

Did you know that in the early stages of fetal development, the brain and the colon start from the same tissue and then split apart? The outcome is two separate nervous systems and, as a result, *two separate brains*. Everyone has both a brain in the head and a brain in the colon (more often referred to as the gut). The body's largest cranial nerve actually keeps these two brains connected, allowing them to communicate back and forth.

It is also a scientific fact that our gut-brain has nearly every controlling chemical as its upward counterpart. These connections explain the physical manifestations resulting from different stresses or emotions as well as the common phrases we all use and hear, such as reference to *gut feelings* or *listening to your gut*. For example, have you ever had butterflies in your stomach before a blind date? Have you ever felt nauseated before an important meeting or felt gut-wrenching pain from a break-up? Now, that puts the term **stinkin' thinkin'** truly into focus.

Within the underlying connection of the brain and gut-brain is the importance of both good emotional and physical health and hence the birth of the **bathirmation** and the bathirming process. Throughout this book, you will find many **pottyisms**. Make these your new words to live by and check out the book's glossary, the **vocrapulary**, for many more. For now, consider the following definitions here:

> **ba•thirm** [buh-**therm**] *vb* : 1) to simultaneously cleanse yourself emotionally and physically while using the toilet or bathroom; 2) to make poositive statements while in the bathroom; 3) to affirm or establish a better state of being through poositive thinking while in the bathroom; 4) to bring in the poositive while flushing away the negative; 5) to connect with your inner self while simultaneously flushing away emotional and physical toxins and waste.
>
> **bath•ir•ma•tion** [bath-er-**mey**-shuhn] *n* : 1) a poositive statement declared while

sitting on the thinking pot; 2) a poositive affirmation made to help enhance an inspirational movement.

What a fantastic way to get your day off to a great start! We consider this book to be the ultimate bathroom book and hope you will too. It's a book that will change your **constipatory** thinking—thoughts that keep you stuck in your ways—into free-flowing, poositive thinking. Your potty routine will never be the same! Intrigued? Feeling moved? Well then, it's time to learn how to get going in the right direction.

This book is designed to be fun, but also to provide inspiration and more than just the usual relief you get while in the bathroom. In fact, it is designed to double your relief by flushing away both the emotional waste and physical waste. So come on, life is a *potty*! Don't worry, **pee happee**. Go with the flow. Allow yourself to be moved.

Remember . . . **&#!+** happens. It's what you do with it that matters!

Be sure you have a pen before starting the next chapter. Go grab it now. Place it in your potty space so it's ready for your next visit.

It's a GASWAR!

or . . .

Grab A Square
Write And Release

Grab
A
Square (toilet paper)
Write down your negative thought, worry, or concern
And
Release it into the toilet bowl.

The foundation of this book is centered on maximizing your time on the porcelain throne by releasing negative emotional energy and attitudes through the **GASWAR** process and by bathirming new poositive energy and attitudes into your life. While we have designed this ritual to symbolize the emotional release, our bodies take care of the physical release of negative energy on a daily basis.

Every day, the human body produces gas and normally releases it by passing the physical energy through your behind. Did you know that the average person produces about one to three pints of gas each day? That's a lot of gas that needs to be passed, or farting to do. The specialists state that, on average, everyone farts fourteen to twenty-three times per day. Wow! That sheds a whole new perspective on GASWARs!

We don't have to tell you how painful it can be when your body doesn't effectively release these toxins. Have you visited the pharmacy or grocery store lately and seen the aisle of products promising to provide relief from the resulting physical discomfort?

There are also numerous **pooscriptions**—or what we call **poo-meds**—out there that promise to provide relief for your emotional pain. We think it is worth noting that emotional distress and build-up also produces toxicity and pain. Pharmaceutical companies are capitalizing on our poor physical and emotional health. Remember, there is a direct connection between emotional turmoil and how it manifests itself physically. It goes right back to fetal development and the brain-gut connection.

So, whether it is a physical gas-war or an emotional GASWAR, it is all about the release of negative energy and its direct correlation to a healthier and happeer you. It's what the GASWAR process and bathirming is all about. Time to get you started on changing the negative inflow into a poospositive outflow.

We all wake up after a long night and need to use the potty; if not immediately, then certainly while we get ready for the day. So as you start your day sitting on the throne, think about what it is that holds you back from living life to its fullest. Is it something you are worried about or fear? Maybe it is the pain you feel from losing something or someone you love. Perhaps it is the loss of a dream. What is it that keeps you stuck in your ways, preventing you from moving forward? Whatever it is, it's time to relieve yourself of the burdensome load (in more ways than one).

As you sit in your private space on your porcelain throne, consider this serene moment as the ultimate time to rid yourself of these negative inflows and replace them with bathirmations. Oh crap! Did you forget the pen? Better get up and go get one.

Now that you are back, simply address an issue that you want to change. Let the GASWAR begin by grabbing a square, writing, and releasing your worry, your fear, or your stumbling block.

For instance, maybe you continue to dwell on what could have been if you had just handled a situation differently. If only you had told someone how you really felt when you had a chance, but now it is too late. Perhaps someone hurt you deeply and you are having a difficult time letting go. Whatever is weighing you down, write it down on that square. For example:

"Peter, you are out of my life, and I'm leaving you right here where you belong!" You can feel safe and free to write down whatever you want. Don't worry. No one else will see it but you—as long as you remember to flush! Congratulations, you just had your first GASWAR.

Now, the next step is to write your new poositive bathirmation in your book. There is a place designed specifically for this part of the process at the end of each chapter. Consider it your **epeephany** of the day! Think about what it is that you want to bathirm for yourself. A bathirmation should be expressed in the present tense: the here and now. Start on a poositive note by beginning your bathirmation with phrases like "I am," "I choose," or "I have." For example, write down "I am worthy of a good relationship" instead of writing "I *will* have a great relationship someday." Remember to keep it in the present tense. Write it as if you already have a wonderful relationship and then believe it. We have included some bathirmations you can choose from or you can create your own.

- Today I let go of the past and embrace the here and now.
- I look forward to this day and all it brings my way.
- I choose to focus on the poositive and to not let life's little hiccups consume me.
- I have the poower to control how I react to life's challenges.

- I believe in myself.
- I cherish life's journey, as there is no dress rehearsal.

Make your bathirmation your mantra for the day. Your day is just beginning and so is the complete bathirmation routine. Today, every time you revisit the bathroom, **repeet** the ritual keeping in sync with the release of physical toxins. We refer to this new daily exercise as **FART**: **F**ollow **A**ffirmation **R**itual **T**hrough as this will enable you to focus and stay conscious of your new Bathirmation of the day. Even if it means replaying the GASWAR out in your head while you finish your physical business, you can still experience the emotional flush in the process. Most importantly, remember your new mantra and bathirm and rebathirm it each and every time—until you believe it. Remember, what happens in there, stays in there so let it rip.

GASWAR, bathirm and FART!

You're ready to get started on your own. The rest of the book includes some inspirational thoughts and bathirmations to help you get moving and motivated. It's time to get rid of the stinkin' thinkin' and move your way into a healthier, happeer and more peaceful you. Remember . . . don't worry, pee happee!

Life is a potty, so don't get left behind!

bathirmations

Your Epeephany of the day . . .
bathirm a new poositive attitude!

Lightening the load continued . . .
more bathirmations and epeephanies.

The "P-Word"

or . . .

There's Nothing Wrong
with Talking about It

When you were a child, did you ever sing the ABC song and skip over the letter P? Do you remember the anticipation of your audience saying "You forgot the P!" only to respond with "No, I didn't . . . it's running down my leg"? Then the chortling and laughter would explode. It's natural for people to giggle in uncomfortable moments. We don't know quite what to say or how to react, so we laugh nervously. It seems to break the tension and get us through those squeamish times. There's nothing like living life on the edge by pushing the envelope and saying the "P-word." Talk about living dangerously.

But why is it that one of our body's most natural functions is such a taboo topic? People get uncomfortable just talking about the excretion process. There are so many euphemisms used in an attempt to be **poolitically correct** that it is ridiculous. Let us present the following examples:

Going . . .

- number one (How did going "number one" become number one?)
- number two (Uh, can't talk about this one—or should we say *two*?)
- potty (This one is a keeper, "baby talk" or not.)
- tinkle (How did a word associated with ringing sounds and music become "baby talk" for peeing? Do you hear music when you tinkle?)
- to the restroom (How is it restful? You're not sleeping in there.)
- to the can (We hope you can.)
- to the john (What does John have to do with this?)
- to the head (Someone must have known about the brain-gut connection on this one.)
- to the porcelain throne (While on the throne, you are definitely in charge.)
- to the thinking pot (Now we're talking!)
- to the crapper (Was Thomas Crapper flattered or appalled?)
- to the toilet (Bullseye!)

What happens in the bathroom is no secret, so why is it so poolitically incorrect and uncomfortable to talk about what is so natural? It is just as essential to life as eating food and sleeping. Yet when we talk about using the toilet, we resort to baby talk, pretense and propriety. Give it up already! Enough is enough.

Our advice: we say quit worrying about being poo-litically correct about it. There is nothing improper about using the toilet or talking about the natural bodily functions. How is it that poolitics works its way into everything anyway? We say poo-poo on that. (By the way, we love our P–words as you will see in all of our pottyisms.)

No matter how you refer to the bathroom ritual, we want you to enhance your task at hand and embrace a whole new potty routine. Use the GASWAR process to release both the emotional and physical **poo** in your life. Make it your time to let down your guard and release your inhibitions.

Grab that square and write down your problem in a sentence or less, for example, "I refuse to let politics control my life!" Now, crumple it up and release it. Throw it in the toilet. That's right; flush it and let it go! There is nothing that can provide greater relief than a GASWAR. Feels great, doesn't it? **Absopoorly!**

Okay, it is now time to bathirm a new poositive approach. We have included some suggested bathirmations below to get you started on the power of positive potty pondering track! Find one that works for you or create your own. Either way, write down your bathirmation at the end of the chapter on your *bathirmations* page. Don't forget to add a few more P–words to your new vocrapulary.

- I breathe out tension and breathe in calm.
- I let go and relax.
- I am important to myself and to others.
- I approach today with passion and purpose.
- I release my burdens and inhibitions.
- I give myself permission to be me.

Remember to FART as many times as you can today—Follow affirmation ritual through! Let your inhibitions go!

bathirmations

Your Epeephany of the day . . .
bathirm a new poositive attitude!

Lightening the load continued . . .
more bathirmations and epeephanies.

Constipatory Thinking

or . . .

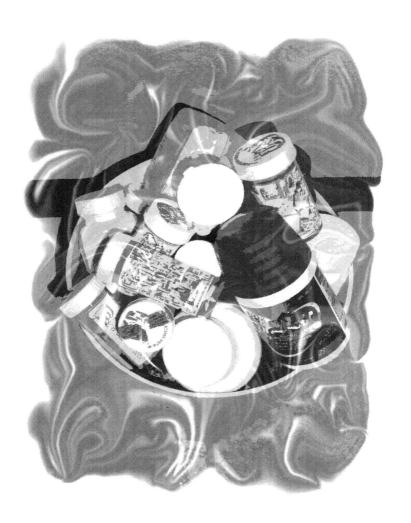

Let Go of the Past

Have you ever been physically constipated and, as a result, felt absolutely miserable? All you desperately wanted was to find relief so you could feel normal again. How did you find relief? For most of us, relief can be found through some form of laxative. There are varying strengths of course, depending on how plugged up we might be, but we all need help at some point or another.

How about your emotional constipation—your constipatory thinking? Maybe you are so consumed by certain thoughts and ideas that you feel sad. Perhaps you can't stop thinking about what could have been if only you had done this or that, leaving yourself stuck in your past and your own self-despair. As a result, it is a challenge to have a *movement* in a forward direction. Why would you think that constipatory thinking can be unplugged on its own? Where is the relief for this misery?

Well, thank goodness you are holding the ultimate pooscription in your hands right now.

Bathirming is the art of cleansing the emotional self. It is the emotional laxative to emotional constipation. Unlike the movie, *Groundhog Day*, you can't change the past, no matter how many times you replay the events over and over. That movie is a good example of trying to overplay things time and time again until things are set right.

You can't go back and change the past, so why stay stuck in it? Imagine waking up each day only to relive the same day over and over in an effort to change the one thing you did wrong. What about all of the moments that you wouldn't have changed? It seems like a waste of time to relive those moments just to wish you would have relived one minute of your day differently.

Of course, we can't really go back in time and change history, but essentially you are wasting precious moments every time you allow yourself to get stuck in the past. You are replacing real moments with emotional moments. You must realize you are only cheating yourself by staying stuck in your negative thought pattern and, in the process, you rob yourself of moving on and living life to its fullest today.

Everyday has its peaks and valleys. There are those superb moments along with ones we would rather forget. Think of it this way: when you watch a movie, read a book, or go to a Broadway play, is everything in the storyline **poofect**? Absopooply not! Wouldn't it be boring if it were?

Life is full of ups and downs. When painful hurts from the past come up, recognize that these are the burdens that need to be healed and released. You can't change the past, but you can work on the here and now. Get rid of those emotional wedgies, and allow yourself to move forward. Time for that GASWAR! Grab a square, write and release.

Write down the emotional load that burdens you. It could be as simple as one word (for example, "Peter!") or the first novel written on toilet paper squares! Use the whole roll if needed. It all depends on how much emotional (and maybe physical) dumping you have to do, but take the time to do it. It's important to your emotional **therapee**.

Time to bathirm what is real. Replace that stinkin' thinkin' and begin anew. Here are some bathirmations below to get the constipatory thinker moving again. If you already have one in mind, feel free to use your own. Whatever you do, don't forget to write down your bathirmation at the end of the chapter on your *bathirmations* page.

- I focus on the future and all of the possibilities life has to offer.
- I am exactly where I am meant to be.
- I learn from my mistakes, and I am better person for them.
- I choose to live in the moment and not to dwell on the past.
- I leave the past behind me where it belongs.

- Today I am back into the game of life, awake and living my dream.
- I give myself permission to wipe away the past and to celebrate this moment.
- I free myself from emotional wedgies!

GASWAR, bathirm and FART. Leave the past behind; live in the here and now.

bathirmations

Your Epeephany of the day . . .
bathirm a new poositive attitude!

Lightening the load continued . . .
more bathirmations and epeephanies.

The Runs

or . . .

Stop Running . . . Slow Down

Imagine that your life is like a roll of toilet paper. Think of each square as a day or moment in time. Each of us needs to take one square at a time. Savor each moment and always spare a moment or square for family and friends.

Do you feel like you are constantly running or on the go? We are all busy, or so we seem to think. On the scale of one to ten, how often do you hear or use excuses like these?

- I've just been really busy.
- I don't have time to do anything fun anymore!
- Passion in life? Who has time for that?
- Sorry I haven't called, but my schedule has been crazy.
- If only I had the time, I could do so much more.
- I wish I could, but things are just too hectic right now.
- I'm really swamped today. How about tomorrow?

It's time to be honest. You might think you are

as busy as a potty at the state fair, but you're not. Moreover, as long as you are immersed in this vicious cycle, tomorrow never really comes. Tomorrow turns out just like today: "really busy." Why do we think we are busier than everybody else to the extent that we don't slow down? We keep running like hamsters on a wheel, running, but really getting nowhere. Ponder, or **poonder**, this thought for a moment. What happens when you take your hand and start spinning the roll of toilet paper from where it **peecefully** rests? The answer is simple! You get a large pile of wasted squares in a tangled mess. Don't waste your moments by spinning yourself out of control.

Take control of your roll—the toilet paper of life. Take each square one at a time. Stop running! Slow down and realize that life is happening while you are busy planning for it. Take time to smell the roses and enjoy each and every square. Realize that there is only today to seize and no promise of any tomorrows.

Time for the GASWAR! Grab that square and write down what is troubling you, for example, "Dang it! I'm not super human! I can't be everything for everybody."

Now, what is your bathirmation for today?

We challenge you to **poogle** (search your inner thoughts) while on the thinking pot. Write your own bathirmation or use one from this list. Either way, write it in your book, make it your own, and believe it! It's time to regain control of your roll!

- Today I seize and appreciate every moment.

- Today I make the things I want to do a priority.
- Today I repeet the success of yesterday.
- I proclaim to just poo it!
- I enjoy every step of life's journey as each step is unique, never to be taken again.
- I savor each and every moment, each and every breath.
- I fill my life with meaning and release the empty words and paralyzing actions.
- Today I make time for my family and friends.

Don't forget to **F**ollow **A**ffirmation **R**itual **T**hrough each time you head to the **head** (more bathroom jargon)! Slow down and savor each and every moment.

bathirmations

Your Epeephany of the day . . .
bathirm a new poositive attitude!

Lightening the load continued . . .
more bathirmations and epeephanies.

The Potty Mouth

or . . .

Poisonous Envy

Do you realize that when you are jealous of another person, it has no reflection on them, but just on you? Jealousy is a reflection of your own self-worth—or, rather, the lack thereof. You've heard the old adage that "the grass is always greener on the other side." Why do you think that is? Well, we'll tell you why. Your neighbors have been bathirming who they are and who they want to be. All of the sludge and crap they have flushed away has helped fertilize their lawns. We all know what makes up fertilizer, and it stinks!

Jealousy has a tendency to turn people into green-eyed monsters. Storing too much fertilizer in both your upper and lower brain maybe? Regardless, the end result turns the green-eyed monster into the green-eyed gossiper. The envy takes on a life of its own and becomes like poison ivy. This toxic transformation stems from your own perception of what is happening next door or even to the people you love and respect the most. Being a gossiper, or potty mouth, may give the sense of momentary gratification and self-worth, but instead does just the opposite. You are only compromising your values and moral compass.

A potty mouth is someone who isn't happee with his or her own life; it really has nothing to do with anyone else. When you put another person down, it is only a subconscious attempt to elevate yourself. By being joyful and happee for someone else, you elevate your own self-worth, not for the moment, but for a lifetime.

So, when you see the green squall of jealousy rolling in and you are not feeling good about yourself, stop blowing wind about others. Don't be a potty mouth. Instead, take a look at yourself and try to find the break in the clouds. Get out from under their ominous dark shadow and shed a poositive light on your own life's lawn.

Now, GASWAR time. Grab that square and write down that colossal load! For example, "I'm done trying to keep up with the Jones!"

Did you remember to release and flush? Great job! Now, it's time to bathirm until your grass is lush and green. Here are some **poossible** bathirmations for you to poogle and to help you get started.

- I fertilize my own lawn instead of trying to kill the lawns of others.
- I allow my life to be joyous and loving.
- I elevate myself by speaking kindly of others.

- I am happee with myself and with others.
- I rise above the desire to engage in diminishing conversations.
- Today is the first of many best days to come.
- I live my passion starting now!

Now FART and focus on fertilizing your own lawn.

bathirmations

Your Epeephany of the day . . .
bathirm a new poositive attitude!

Lightening the load continued . . .
more bathirmations and epeephanies.

Wipe It; Wipe It Good

or . . .

Forgiveness

There is no doubt that forgiveness is a tricky concept for many of us and can be a difficult thing to do. To forget is nearly impossible, but it's really about letting go and leaving the past where it belongs. This does not mean that you are condoning what happened to you, but instead refuse to accept it as a toxic influence in your life. By not forgiving, you will continue to hold onto bitterness and resentment and remain victim to the painful memories. Large amounts of energy are used by holding on to anger, fear, shame and sadness. Holding on can weaken you and make you more susceptible to illness and depression. Forgiveness will allow you to detach from the venom left by your offender. Remember— not forgiving someone is like taking a poison pill and hoping the other person dies.

There is no doubt that forgiveness is a tricky concept for many of us and can be a difficult thing to do. On the other hand, forgetting may seem nearly impossible, but it's really about letting go and leaving the past where it belongs. By not forgiving, you continue to hold onto an element of bitterness and remain victim to the painful memories. Although the memories are stored away, you can free yourself from a life sentence of agony and bitterness. Don't anchor yourself to the anguish. Do you really want to hang onto something that brought you pain in the first place?

No matter what your reasons are for hanging onto bitterness and not letting go, you do have the choice. You can release yourself from negative thoughts, actions, and energy. Take a stand and set healthy boundaries. Forgiveness doesn't mean you will let people continue to hurt you. Instead, it means making a liberating choice and allowing yourself to be free of the baggage that would otherwise continue to haunt you.

When you decide to forgive, you take back control of your life. You set your own limitations. Only you are responsible for your own feelings, so don't relinquish your poower. We challenge you to rethink forgiveness. You are really only hurting yourself. You need to wipe it and wipe it good—in other words, choose forgiveness.

You know what you need to do next! It's time for your daily GASWAR. Write down what you are having a hard time wiping out of your mind and let it go, for example, "Peter, you are still haunting me, and I'm done with you!" Now, release that square and let forgiveness flush it away.

Once again, it's time to bathirm. Here are some suggested bathirmations to help you truly wipe away your burden today and to wipe it, and wipe it good! Use another square if needed.

- I choose to forgive and to take back the poower and control of my life.
- I give myself the gift of forgiveness so I can move into the realm of understanding.
- I lose more weight in a single day than physically poossible by just forgiving and letting go.
- I free myself from resentful and bitter thoughts.
- I experience loving and healthy relationships.

Now forgive and don't forget to FART!

bathirmations

Your Epeephany of the day . . .
bathirm a new poositive attitude!

Lightening the load continued . . .
more bathirmations and epeephanies.

The Thirty-Second-Recharge

or . . .

There's Plenty of Time to Be Positive

L et's face it. Some moments on the pot last less than thirty seconds. Regardless, there is still enough time to flush away a worry and to bathirm what is truly **impootant**.

Who says bathirming needs to be complicated and inconvenient? Even if you only have thirty seconds, there is still time to bathirm. We call it the *thirty-second-recharge*. Here are thirty-one bathirmations to help give you that emotional recharge when your throne and alone times are limited. This gives you one for every day of the month. Let this chapter serve as your daily vitamin for the emotional soul. You can refer to it each and every day or when you're stuck and need some bathirmation ideas. Whatever you do, don't forget to have your GASWAR first (e.g., "I'm so done with you Peter and feel free!"—though we're not trying to pick on the Peters out there). Then pick your bathirmation or write your own. Remember to write it down on your *bathirmations* page and bathirm it until you believe it!

- I am a perceptive and intuitive human being.
- I stay balanced and centered.
- I live in the now and do not dwell on the past.
- I let go of the past and live only for today.
- I am at peece with my own feelings.
- I believe in myself.
- I crack a smile for what I have instead of crying about what I've lost.
- I am capable of doing anything I set my mind to doing.
- I listen to my gut, as it is my back-up brain.
- Today I embrace my life and bow out of the manic race going nowhere.
- Today I praise my family, convey their worth to me, and express how much I appreciate them.
- Today I call an old friend and make room for a new one.
- I acknowledge my own mortality so I can appreciate every moment for the experience it brings.
- I fill my day with poositive and forward thinking thoughts.
- I cherish life's journey, as there is no dress rehearsal.
- I am strong and capable; I love being me.
- I understand life is about change, so I am open-minded and adaptable.
- I enjoy and appreciate the beauty of that which surrounds me.

- I am off of the one-way road headed for self-destruction and hit the freeway to self-fulfillment.
- I am worthy of giving love and being loved.
- I rejoice in the here and now and stop punishing myself.
- I can do anything because I believe in myself.
- I have so much to give, and I share it with joy.
- I love life and am blessed with the one that I have.
- I pledge to keep things in perspective by FARTing.
- I do not waste time on things that are beyond my control.
- I choose to let my experiences be happee and poositive.
- I am not afraid of change; I welcome the diversion.
- I stay out of my own way of finding happeeness.
- I let go of private pity parties and focus on my blessings.
- I am my own best friend, not my own worst enemy.
- I graduate to president of my own fan club.

No matter what happens today, remember to continue with your new ritual and FART.

bathirmations

Your Epeephany of the day . . .
bathirm a new poositive attitude!

Lightening the load continued . . .
more bathirmations and epeephanies.

Don't Worry, Pee Happee

or . . .

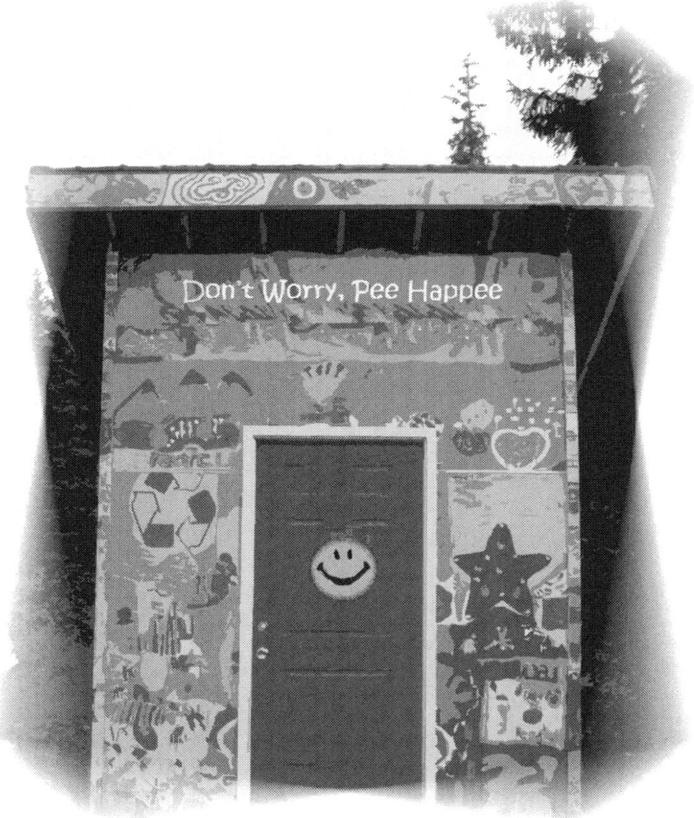
Don't Worry, Pee Happee

Leave Your Worries Behind

Are you a worrywart? Is it helping you or just making your day-to-day life more miserable? If you are like the rest of us, you recognize that it isn't doing anything but causing undue stress and sleepless nights. Worrying can become so intertwined in our lives that it takes on a life of its own.

This infringing creature infiltrates our personal relationships, financial world, and work environment and distorts our perspective. It manages to play games with both of our brains: the one that rests in the skull and the other that is coiled in the torso. You fall victim to mind tricks and a somersaulting gut.

Worry is an attempt to control the future or change the past, neither of which you can do. All of us tend to over think things at times. We fret over an "at risk" relationship or career. We worry about our health or the health of a loved one. We can't stop living and reliving conversations in our minds. We worry about something we said or didn't say, or we stress over what we should or shouldn't do next.

There is a little poem that you may have heard multiple versions of over the years. No one knows the source, and it has been modified multiple times. Here is one small rendition of it:

Worry never climbed a hill.
Worry never paid a bill.
Worry never dried a tear.
Worry never claimed a fear.
Worry never led a horse to water.
Worry never did a thing it oughta!

—Anonymous

As simplistic as that might seem, it captures the reality poofectly. Whether it is concern about a perceived problem in the past, present, or future, worrying about it will not solve anything. It is a waste of energy and this little book is all about getting rid of that excess waste.

Only you can choose to stop being consumed with worry. Don't worry, pee happee! **Dispoose** of the worrisome attitude—the **worritude**—and flush it away. What is it that is weighing you down today? Time to lighten the load. GASWAR time. Grab that square and write down your worry and release. Flush it; flush it good!

Now, it's time to find a bathirmation to make your mantra for the day. We have included some bathirmations for you to poogle. Maybe you already have a new one in mind for today, or you might have one that still needs repeeting. Whatever the case may be, bathirm your way to a new poositive state of mind. Don't forget to write it on your *bathirmations* page and repeet it until you believe it. Work on **empoowering** yourself. Make it your own.

- Today I wipe out the past, trust in the future, and rejoice in the magnificent now.
- I need not worry for I am protected by a divine source.
- I trust that all is well and works towards my good.
- I stay in the now and do not dwell on the past.
- I release the past and live only for today.
- I celebrate the here and now and stop punishing myself.
- I excrete nothing but poositive energy.
- I find happeeness by staying out of my own way.

Don't worry, pee happee. Remember to keep on FARTing and leave your worries behind.

bathirmations

Your Epeephany of the day . . .
bathirm a new poositive attitude!

Lightening the load continued . . .
more bathirmations and epeephanies.

Sometimes You Feel Like a Dump; Sometimes You Don't

or . . .

You Are Worthy

There are many of us that have experienced the pain of rejection or betrayal. Whether it is from a broken heart or a lost friendship, the sting can be all consuming and overwhelming. This particular matter can be very difficult to release. Every fiber of our being seems to be affected by complications from the emotion called love. We internalize this ache and tend to hold onto it until it wreaks havoc on our self-worth. You wonder, "Why did he leave? Was I not good enough?" "What went wrong?" you ask yourself. "Was it my fault?"

When it comes to matters of the heart, unfortunately, things don't always go our way. It is our choice to use this experience to grow no matter how difficult it might seem. When love relationships go smoothly, we feel blessed, as if Cupid stays with us long after the arrow is launched. When our hearts get broken, we feel abandoned. It's as though Cupid missed the target altogether. The truth is that we are blessed in both cases, although it may not seem like it in the midst of the heart-wrenching trauma. Think of it this way: maybe you are being prepared for the arrival of Mr. or Ms. Right. Whether you like it or not, maybe it is time to let go.

Additionally, when things go wrong in a friendship that has been a major force in your life, it can be devastating. You can be left feeling bewildered, again taking on guilt and wondering what could have been done differently to maintain the status quo. The underlying truth is that sometimes the status quo isn't the best state.

Life is ever changing; nothing remains status quo for long. People change, but that is not to say that all relationships—whether in love or in friendship—fizzle when hit with the relationship chisel. Many survive the most difficult of storms and become stronger as a result. Sometimes, no matter what you try to do, there is nothing you can do to save the sizzle from the fizzle-smashing-chisel. Change is not the end but is instead a new beginning. It is all in how you decide to embrace the change and seize what is to follow.

Poonder this next thought.

Love is never really lost if it was real in the first place. Maybe it wasn't yours to keep. The same can be said for friendships. If you truly, deeply love and care for a person, you don't let go of that. If you find that you are the *dumpee*, reset your internal barometer and know that maybe life has something different and better in store for you. Just have faith in yourself and believe that the pain you feel now will be replaced with joy, love, and friendship again. You are not alone on this journey; it is part of the process, or **poocess**, of life. Yes, love can hurt, but wouldn't it hurt more to go through life without love at all? Follow your heart and do not be afraid to trust and love again.

It's now time to GASWAR, bathirm, and FART. Remember to write down your concern and dump the load. It is impootant that you express your pain and feelings. The expression itself is healing. Now, crumple it up and release it by flushing it away. Ahhh . . . what unbelievable relief! It's time to follow up with a bathirmation or two. Here are some for you to poogle, or you can bathirm one of your own. Either way, write it in your book and integrate it into your daily routine, or **pootine**.

- I am worthy of love and all of the divine pleasures that it brings my way.
- I am a love machine; love comes to me easily.
- I attract my poofect soul mate.
- I accept all that love has to offer.
- I surrender completely to the moments of today, and I enjoy each one to its fullest.
- I am responsible for my own life.
- I vow at this moment to live in the here and now.
- I fill today with the things that move me toward progress and peece.

Remember, GASWAR, bathirm and FART!

bathirmations

Your Epeephany of the day . . .
bathirm a new poositive attitude!

Lightening the load continued . . .
more bathirmations and epeephanies.

Here a Crap, There a Crap, Everywhere a Crap, Crap

or . . .

It's Always Something

oes it feel like everything around you is going wrong? Does "Murphy's law" (what can go wrong, will go wrong) always come down on you? Maybe you expect or anticipate things to run amok, and it has now become a self-fulfilling prophecy.

Why are you surprised? If you expected it, then you got exactly what you expected! You reap what you sow. When you plant your mind with crap, crap is what you harvest. If you want to eliminate the crap around you, quit planting the seeds. Try this approach instead: expect things to go your way and see what happens. The mind is a poowerful thing and thoughts, whether poositive or negative, carry the poower. Replace the negative or stinkin' thinkin' with the poositive. Start believing that good things can and will happen.

What is your passion in life? Do you have dreams for yourself? Sometimes life is so full of menial and dutiful tasks that you go through the motions but feel no emotion. Allow more flexibility in your daily pootine to awaken your deep-rooted interest and seize the day. **Car*POO* Diem!** Stop putting off your happeeness today for a promise of it being there tomorrow.

Wipe away those cobwebs and explore your dreams. Make them your reality by acting on each and every today that comes your way. We are blessed with twenty-four hours in a day. You are impootant enough to take some of that time just for you. Don't assume tomorrow will be there. We are not promised any moments beyond the current one we're living in. Make each one count.

Be content with what you have and quit hanging your happeeness on what you don't have. Grab that square right now and write down your negative baggage. Let it flow from your mind and out of your body through the pen in your hand. Now you have two elimination systems working for you!

It's that time again and you know what to do: GASWAR and bathirm. Be sure to flush it and flush it good. Feel the sense of freedom as you watch your cares disappear in the toilet's tornado.

What is your bathirmation today? Think about it and make it your own. Repeet as many times as necessary until you believe it enough to live it. Here are some anti-clogging bathirmations to help you dispoose of the mental waste and to get you moving in the right direction. Remember to journal it on your *bathirmations* page.

- I make time to do what is impootant to me today.
- I am the only one that controls my happeeness.
- I find my happeeness in the here and now instead of waiting for it to find me.
- Today I convert my dreams into my reality.
- I count my blessings no matter how small they seem.
- I find time and space to cultivate my passion.
- I find balance between going through the motions and feeling emotions.

Here a FART, there a FART . . . everywhere a FART, FART! Continue your daily mantra.

bathirmations

Your Epeephany of the day . . .
bathirm a new poositive attitude!

Lightening the load continued . . .
more bathirmations and epeephanies.

When You Gotta Go, You Gotta Go!

or . . .

Find Your Backbone!

Ouch! That hurt! Have you ever found yourself struggling in a relationship that is going nowhere—a situation where you find yourself giving and giving and the other person taking and taking, sapping you of all your energy? Maybe a friend betrayed you or a business partner lied to you. Poossibly you are married to someone who prefers to ride the wide-open range rather then spend time with you in front of the home fires.

You find yourself in a vulnerable position. You finally open your heart, and then zing! Here comes the bullet! Shot after shot you take the bullets, occasionally dodging a few, but soon again finding yourself as someone else's target.

When you gotta go, you gotta go!

When you find yourself in a relationship that is abusive and hurtful, it is time to get out. This can be complicated to do when you have already jumped in with both feet. It is difficult to let go. Self-esteem is at an all time low. You often think that what these people say and do to hurt you must be your fault and somehow you deserve it. You don't! It is absopooply time to go!

Take your feet out of the quicksand that threatens to swallow you alive. You have the poower, and you have the choice. You must believe in yourself and need to remember that you are worth it. It is essential that you don't let anyone make you feel otherwise. Face your offender. Start standing up for yourself, and stop allowing that person to hurt you.

Remember, you can't control how someone behaves towards you, but you can control how you react to it. Is the offensive behavior okay with you? If it is, why are you feeling so insignificant, unworthy, and dissatisfied? If it isn't okay, it's time to put the pedal to the metal and say goodbye to dysfunction junction. Immediately proceed to the first exit ramp, metaphorically speaking. Never allow anyone to control you and your emotions; only you can do that.

It's time to GASWAR. You know what you need to do. Write it down, for example, "See you later, Peter!" and flush it away. Dump the load!

Now, here are some bathirmations designed to reinforce what you already know, because when you gotta go, you gotta go!

- I am worthy of love and happeeness.
- I am in control of how I react to a situation and how I feel.

- I am responsible for my emotions, and only I control them.
- I have the poower to change my life.
- I deserve happee and healthy relationships.

Remember to **F**ollow **A**ffirmation **R**itual **T**hrough every time you gotta go!

bathirmations

Your Epeephany of the day . . .
bathirm a new poositive attitude!

Lightening the load continued . . .
more bathirmations and epeephanies.

It's Time to Crack a Smile

or . . .

Don't Put Bliss on Hold

What is happeeness? The standard definition is:

hap·pee·ness [ha-pee-nis] n : 1) the state of being happee; 2) good fate, blissfulness, gratification, joyfulness.

"The state of being happee." What is it that makes you happee? Perhaps you find yourself saying "I'll be happee when . . .

- I get that new job offer."
- I can get a bigger house."
- I can finally buy that new convertible."
- I _____ (fill in your blank)."

What do you seem to think you need that is keeping you from being happee right now? It is poossible to find happeeness while in the **poosuit** of happeeness. Don't put bliss on hold.

Look around you right now. Well, maybe right now isn't the time, but maybe it is. There are so many things to be happee about if you make an effort to look. Are you in the privacy of your own space? Do you have shelter, warmth, and toilet paper? Can you read and write? Don't take these things for granted, as many people aren't even fortunate enough to have what you might consider ordinary.

Think about that for a moment.

We are sure you can add to the list of "little" everyday things that you are thankful for but don't always appreciate. When you woke up this morning, maybe you weren't looking forward to your day, but at least you have another day to live and poosue your dreams.

Challenge yourself today to look around and be grateful for all of the things you have now that make you happee no matter how small or simple they might seem. You know what they say: sometimes the best things come in the smallest and simplest of packages. We all get in our own little rut, but we need to snap out of it. Don't wait to grab the carrot you dangle in front of yourself before you can be happee.

It's a choice. Choose to be happee right now that you even have the opportunity to poosue the carrot. Quit hanging your happee hat on the end of the poosuit; the point is to be happee during the journey. When you reach your goal, it will be that much sweeter.

Time to GASWAR and then bathirm your new poositive approach for today. As always, here are some suggestions. Remember to work your new mantra into your day, and bathirm it until you believe it.

- I am thankful for my many blessings.
- Today I appreciate life's simplest of pleasures.
- I am blessed and blissed, but certainly not pissed.
- Today I choose to be happee while in the poosuit of happeeness.
- I am grateful for the toilet paper, no matter what brand.
- I am grateful to greet another day, and I do it blissfully (not pissfully).
- I am thankful for the opportunity to experience all of life.

FART, and be sure to crack a smile.

bathirmations

Your Epeephany of the day . . .
bathirm a new poositive attitude!

Lightening the load continued . . .
more bathirmations and epeephanies.

Poo It Forward

or . . .

You Can Always Spare a Square

There is no greater blessing than to have the opportunity to make a difference in someone else's life. From the simplest to the grandest of gestures, what may be insignificant to you can actually make a world of difference to someone else. By giving to another and by pooing it forward, an endless cycle of love is created.

Pooing it forward is like throwing a stone into a pond. That simple action creates a ripple effect. The energy flows outwardly from the point of impact and spreads to everything around it. Happeeness is meant to be shared, not kept to yourself. It's contagious and infectious. You reap what you sow; you get what you give away. How can you give back what you have learned and poo it forward? Here are some simple suggestions from an endless list:

- Smile at a stranger.
- Volunteer at a retirement home.
- Call someone today that you haven't spoken to for

years. Maybe your voice is what they need to hear.

- Give the gift of time.

Pooing it forward can also be a great way to give yourself a lift. Instead of focusing on your own problems, and wallowing in your own self-pity, deflect that negative energy and convert it into something poositive. Perhaps there is someone you know that needs a thirty-second-recharge, or someone that needs to crack a smile.

Maybe a friend needs help learning to wipe it or wipe it good. You can potentially help that constipatory thinker get unstuck and move forward again. Perhaps it could be as simple as passing along the GASWAR philosophy. Whatever the case may be, we hope this little book is doing some or all of that for you. It has without a doubt helped us, and as we poo it forward, we hope it helps you and others. It's another ripple in the pond.

Staying in sync with your new pootine, it is again time to take today's weighty load and let it go. You know what to do. Grab that square, write, and release. Allow yourself to let go and welcome the freedom it brings. Now challenge yourself and others to poo it forward, starting today.

Here are some bathirmations to help aim you in the right direction and to get you pooing it forward. Use your *bathirmations* page to write your own ideas on how to poo it forward, and just poo it today!

- I give freely, unconditionally, and with love.

- I make a difference in someone else's world just by being me.
- I am the stone in the rippling pond of life.
- I open my heart to new poossibilities and welcome the abundance it brings.
- It is my privilege and responsibility to give back and to watch the domino effect take place.

Don't forget to FART and always poo it forward. It's absopooply worth it!

bathirmations

Your Epeephany of the day . . .
bathirm a new poositive attitude!

Lightening the load continued . . .
more bathirmations and epeephanies.

Epeelogue

We would like to polish this voyage off with a few impootant things to remember as you venture out and continue this journey on your own. Remember, everyday our bodies take care of the physical release of negative energy by passing gas, farting, etc., but what about the emotional release? This is where *The Power of Positive Potty Pondering: Bathirmations* takes over. It centers on releasing negative emotional energy and attitudes through the GASWAR poocess and bathirming new poositive energy and attitude into your life.

Whether it is a physical gas-war or an emotional GASWAR, bathirming is all about the release of negative energy and its direct correlation to a healthier and happeer you. It's what the GASWAR poocess and bathirming is all about. How many times do you go to the bathroom in a day? We challenge you to GASWAR, bathirm, and FART every time you do. The more FARTing you do, the more relief you will feel!

We hope this book has opened your mind and thoughts to a new and healthier attitude. We've endeavored to make it a thought-provoking poocess for you and hope it has changed your ordinary daily potty times into an extraordinary bathirming pootine. Can you honestly think of any better use of time spent while on the porcelain throne?

Maybe there is some symbolism here after all. This is the time of your day where you are totally in complete control of your domain. You are sovereign of your thoughts—the only one with the poower to be in command of them. You have the supremacy to turn away from the negative and seize the poositive.

This book was designed to get you moving in the right direction. It was meant to help you refocus your energies and take the reigns back. Car*POO* Diem! Seize the whole day, not just the moments alone on the throne, but every last square of life. Remember, poositive words and thoughts are empoowering. Think yourself into better mental and physical health. Think it, bathirm it, and believe it. Make it your own.

We encourage you to continue this pootine and journey. Keep those GASWARs going! Get rid of that constipatory stinkin' thinkin'. If you find yourself on that hamster wheel, make sure you take the time for at least a thirty-second-recharge. Continue to aim yourself in the right direction, and allow yourself to be moved. Take time to crack a smile. Never forget to spare a square, and always poo it forward.

Don't worry, pee happee!

Remember, **&#!+** happens! It's what you do with it that matters. Let it be your fertilizer to a healthier and happeer life!

Last but not least . . . don't forget to FART! Although this is the end of the book, let it be your new beginning.

Vocrapulary

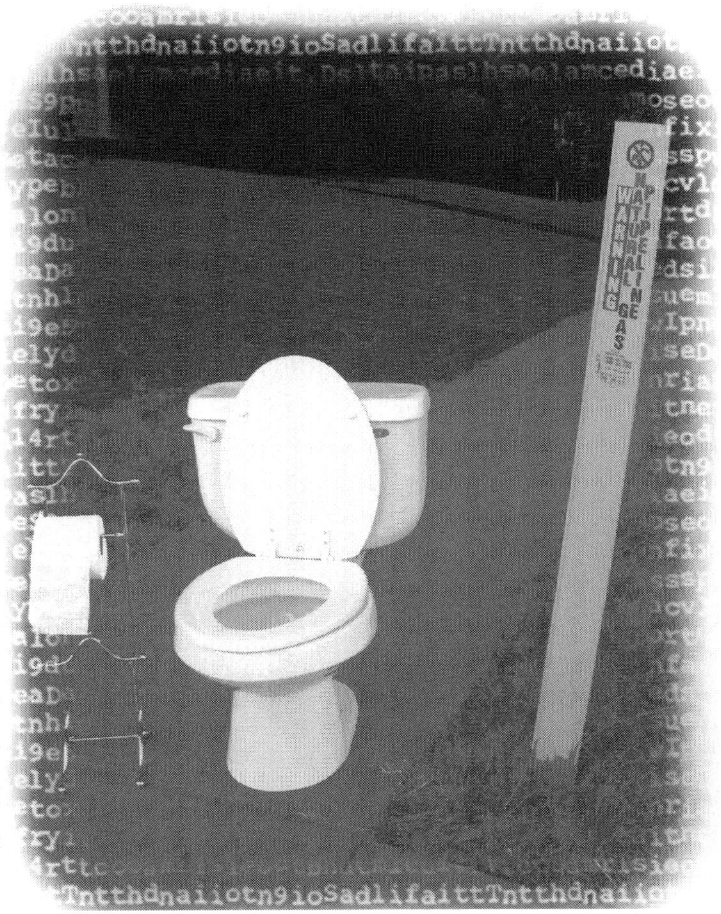
WARNING
GAS
PIPELINE

ab•so•poop•ly [ab-**suh**-poop-lee] *adv* : 1) poositively;
2) without exception, completely, wholly, entirely;
3) certainly, unquestionably.

af•fir•ma•tion [af-er-**mey**-shuhn] *n* : 1) a confirming
statement; 2) a statement or proposition that is
declared to be true; 3) a poositive assertion.

ba•thirm [buh-**therm**] *vb* : 1) to simultaneously
cleanse yourself emotionally and physically while
using the toilet or bathroom; 2) to make poositive
statements while in the bathroom; 3) to affirm or
establish a better state of being through poositive
thinking while in the bathroom; 4) to bring in the
poositive while flushing away the negative; 5) to
connect with your inner self while simultaneously
flushing away emotional and physical toxins and
waste.

bath•ir•ma•tion [bath-er-**mey**-shuhn] *n* : 1) a
poositive statement declared while sitting on the
thinking pot; 2) a poositive affirmation made to help
enhance an inspirational movement.

car•poo di•em [kar-**pooh** dee-um] *imperative phrase* : 1) to seize the day; 2) to enjoy life.

con•sti•pa•tory [**kon**-stuh-puh-tory] *adj* : 1) having an emotional wedgie; 2) being stuck, trapped, or immobilized.

dis•poose [dis-spoohz] *vb* : 1) to release (e.g., "I am ready to dispoose of my negative thoughts"); 2) to get rid of, discard; 3) to destroy.

e•pee•logue [e-**pee**-log] *n* : conclusion to rewarding potty pootine.

e•peeph•a•ny [e-**peef**-uh-nee] *adj* : 1) a sudden and intuitive perception or insight; 2) a moment of revelation and understanding.

em•poo•wer [em-**pooh**-er] *vb* : to take on poower and control.

FART [fahrt] *n* : 1) intestinal gas released by the body; *acronym* : 2) stands for "follow affirmation ritual through."

GAS•WAR [**gas**-wohr] *acronym* : 1) stands for "grab a square, write, and release"—the act of grabbing a square, writing, and releasing your negative thoughts and feelings.

hap•pee [ha-**pee**] *adj* : 1) pleased or blissful; 2) content; 3) delighted.

head [hed] *n* : 1) a toilet onboard a boat or ship; 2) potty; 3) bathroom.

im•poo•tant [im-**pooh**-tent] *adj* : 1) noteworthy; 2) significant; 3) momentous.

pee [pee] *vb* : 1) to be (e.g., "don't worry pee happee"); 2) the act of urinating.

peece [pees] *n* : 1) an inner feeling of contentment (e.g., "I am at peece with myself"); 2) the state of shared harmony between people, especially in personal relationships.

poo [pooh] *n* : 1) waste or excess baggage; 2) negative thoughts; *vb* : 3) to do (e.g., "just poo it"); 4) to pay (e.g., "poo it forward").

poo•cess [**pooh**-sess] *n* : the journey from start to finish.

poo•fect [**pooh**-fekt] *adj* : 1) entirely without blemish, fault or limitation; 2) when something absopooply fits the need in a certain situation or for a certain purpose; 3) exact, correct, or right in every way (e.g., "a poofect time to bathirm").

poo•gle [**pooh**-gull] *vb* : 1) to search your inner thoughts while on the thinking pot; 2) to poonder your options once defined; 3) to seek out the right answer; 4) to consider.

poo•li•ti•cal•ly cor•rect [**pooh**-li-ti-cul-lee **kuh**-rekt] *adv* : 1) using euphemisms to avoid talking about natural bodily functions so as not to offend; 2) changing or avoiding language that might offend anyone, especially with respect to gender, race, or ethnic background.

poo•med [**pooh**-med] *n* : 1) medicine; 2) slang for pooscription.

poon·der [**poohn**-der] *vb* : 1) to think over carefully and thoroughly; 2) to reflect with care and much thought.

poo•scrip•tion [pooh-**skrip**-shuhn] *n* : 1) solution; 2) needed action to fix a problem—also known as poo-med.

poos•si•ble [**poohs**-uh-bull] *adj* : 1) very probable; 2) very likely to happen or become real.

poos•i•tive [**pooh**-zi-tiv] *adj* : 1) undeniably confirmed or promising (e.g., "poositive thinking can make dreams a reality"); 2) confident and self-assured in belief or bathirmation.

poo•sue [**pooh**-soo] *vb* : 1) to do your best to gain; 2) strive to achieve or bring about a purpose, a result, or goal; 3) to move forward with a pootine or plan of action, etc.; 4) to persist or continue.

poo•suit [**pooh**-soot] *n* : 1) an attempt to reach or achieve something of impootence (e.g., "the poosuit of happeeness"); 2) the act of poosuing; 3) mission.

poo•tine [pooh-**teen**] *n* : 1) a regular or habitual way of doing something (e.g., "your daily bathirmation pootine"); 2) a typical or everyday activity; 3) ordinary duties or responsibilities to be done on a regular basis.

poo•wer [**pooh**-er] *n* : 1) capacity to do something or to take action; 2) the ability to accomplish; 3) drive, strength, vitality.

pot•ty•ism [**paw**-tee-iz-um] *n* : 1) a new poositive vocrapulary; 2) word pertaining to bathirmation jargon; 3) bathroom talk.

re•peet [ree-**peet**] *vb* : 1) to say again; 2) to do or make again.

stink•in' think•in' [**stingk**-en thingk-en] *n* : 1) bad thoughts; 2) negative thinking.

ther•a•pee [**ther**-uh-pee] *n* : 1) healing poower or poocess; 2) rehabilitating treatment.

tin•kle [teen-kuhl] *vb* : 1) to go to the bathroom; 2) to go potty.

wor•ri•tude [**wuhr**-ee-tood] *n* : 1) attitude consumed with anxiety and worry; 2) a tormented feeling or condition; 3) worried demeanor.

About the Authors

Lisa Z is a Spiritual and Life Empowerment Coach. A graduate of Holistic Learning Centers, she is a certified Advance Life Skills Coach and Spiritual Life Coach.

Lisa is a long-time student of one's creative powers over the mindset. Like each of us, she is on her own journey of self-discovery. She believes that the thoughts, fears, and joys, which make up our daily lives, influence the state of our physical and emotional health.

Lisa was born and raised in the Pacific Northwest. Over the years, she has written numerous children's stories as well as music and lyrics to songs she has recorded in Los Angeles, Nashville and Portland, Oregon. A true advocate for helping others, Lisa volunteers at her church and has also hosted numerous fundraisers for at-risk children.

Lisa resides in Camas, Washington with her husband and daughter.

Michelle Lang spent most of her life in the Pacific Northwest. During her childhood, she had the experience of living abroad. This opportunity taught her that regardless of physical, spiritual, or cultural differences, we are all on a similar journey: to seek and find happiness. She strongly believes everyone is born with the right to be respected and that we need to embrace our worldly differences, open our hearts and minds, and learn from others.

Although her career has been in the business world, her true passion has been writing musical lyrics, children stories and inspirational essays on the side. Believing that you only live once, she is pursuing a dream by finally turning her passion, creative outlet and hobby into her mainstream focus. Like Lisa, Michelle enjoys giving back to the community through volunteer work. She is an advocate for paying it forward and an avid believer that actions truly speak louder than words.

Michelle lives in the suburbs of Seattle with her husband and two children.

Made in the USA
Charleston, SC
18 November 2016